Praise for GRAY MARKET

I am hooked on Languell's poetry. Her startling shifts among registers of language, her acute prosody, and her savage plain-spokenness reveal not only a great poetic talent but a mind that inquiring people will want to keep close.

-Ann Starr

Gray Market is an unauthorized communiqué from the pneumatic tubes of "tiny little workers without power" to the state, the agencies, the producers and consumers (of folly), and the people of the United States. Depending on who you are, you'll either feel antagonized or incredibly inspired to never again settle for the "stopgap sex act." The antagonized poet pushes back realizing she has (and we have) demanded too little. Krystal Languell's work makes me evermore committed to stay with her on the job, as Poet, where the job is to hack up shit language and redeploy it to make more room for the living.

-Stacy Szymaszek

In single cigarettes sold on a city sidewalk, in "not for individual sale" samples of drugs or beauty products hawked on the Internet, a gray economy blossoms all around us rerouting traditional channels of production and distribution. Krystal Languell's poems outline how individuals thrive and fail such shadowy markets: "When I was working 60 hours a week," she writes, "my dad seemed to like hearing about it." In a personal accounting of employment histories, relationships, workplaces and homes ("The known spaces/that however fucked are familiar"), Languell records the colliding forces of economics, gender, and aesthetics. The vital poems in *Gray Market* reveal and rewire capitalism's circuits of shame and desire. "I am basically begging for it," Languell writes, "but it is/ the revolution not what you imagine I need."

-Susan Briante

In Krystal Languell's *Gray Market*, an abject sensitivity bound up with a crackling, observation-based diction and a nervy, existential wit unpredictably spreads across sharp-edged lines and turns. Languell's poems discretely change form based on the sounds, strands and shards of experience she collects and finds motion within. Those forms are never interchangeable, be they handling the deadpan bank ad's bad language or the seemingly endless array of paradoxical contortions our obsession with assessment demands we constantly perform. Consequently, a disarmingly approachable – and bluntly human – space gets made in this book, one filled with the force and scale of everyday life.

-Anselm Berrigan

GRAY MARKET

Krystal Languell

GRAY MARKET

Krystal Languell

1913 Press
www.1913press.org
1913press@gmail.com

1913 is a not-for-profit collective. Contributions to 1913 Press may be tax-deductible.

Manufactured in the oldest country in the world, The United States of America.

Many thanks to all the artists, from this century and the last, who made this project possible.

Founder & Editrice: Sandra Doller
Vice-Editor: Ben Doller
Managing Editrixes: Adam Bishop & Kim Koga
Designer: Sarah Gzemski

Cover art: Jeffrey Pethybridge

ISBN: 978-0-9906332-7-3

ACKNOWLEDGMENTS

Poems in this manuscript have previously appeared, often in different versions and under different titles in *The Doris, N/A Lit Journal, The Destroyer, esque, inter|rupture, About Place Journal, SET, Columbia Poetry Review, ILK, Puerto del Sol, La Fovea, YEW, The Awl, Two Serious Ladies, Barn Owl Review, Dressing Room, Open Letters, Coconut* and *Similar Peaks.* Thank you to the editors of these publications.

Thank you: Virginia Center for the Creative Arts and the Vermont Studio Center, where portions of this manuscript were composed or revised in 2013; Pratt Institute's Faculty Development Fund in 2015; the Belladonna* Collaborative members, authors, interns, and volunteers, especially Jae Cornick, Saretta Morgan, Chialun Chang, Barbara Henning, Marcella Durand, Jennifer Firestone, Rachel Levitsky, Bill Mazza, Emily Skillings, HR Hegnauer, Caroline Crumpacker, R. Erica Doyle, LaTasha N. Nevada Diggs, Tonya M. Foster and Betsy Fagin for crucial cheer and unconditional love; Stacy Szymaszek, Anselm Berrigan, The Poetry Project and the Jerome Foundation for the support of their Emerge-Surface-Be fellowship program in 2013-2014, and to the Lower Manhattan Cultural Council, where I was a workspace resident in 2014-2015; Guy Pettit for publishing a portion of this collection as the chapbook/poster *Fashion Blast Quarter* with Flying Object in 2014; Elizabeth Clark Wessel for likewise publishing a portion of this collection as the chapbook *Be a Dead Girl* with Argos Books in 2014; Carmen Giménez Smith, my dear friend; Dan Ogorzalek, my person.

GRAY MARKET

CONTENTS

Pain Theory

you reveal my dynamic monologue
a personal will is developing you
not as concise, I become inner
which I very pussy really

which pussy is not dynamic?
my very personal reveal
you become monologue, concise
as I will, a really inner you

to reveal pussy is very personal
really become a monologue
my concise dynamic
as inner, which you will

dynamic as you become
which is really my will
a concise monologue to reveal
personal you, very inner pussy

Get Disappointed

get this hollow spine to undulate. flex in the mirror.
swallow a painkiller. soft light on my sunken cheeks.
nothing like a dream. message against all utility. recovering
the bad words. precocity rewarded. airbrush a so-called
scandal. makeup transforms drab ponytail squad.

planted in kimonos. outraged and feminine yearning in the
pastoral. banal collarbone essence. a budding soundtrack.
dusks. uniformity cut. costuming as defense mechanism.
a subculture. torrent of nature's processes. the majestic
horizon a mockery. the usual mirage of freedom. sparkle.

Catalogue of Humiliations

throwing rocks at cars
throwing snowballs at strangers
throwing trash out of a moving schoolbus
having a chair pulled out from under my feet
prying up the crumbling edge of my street
being told to put the chunk of asphalt back
spitting in another girl's hair
lying when another girl asked me "Are you a Christian?"
arranging the desks so I'd sit next to boys
my mother in the ER
a hot chocolate mug that plugs into the wall socket
puking on every holiday for a lot of years
Easter going home in a blanket, vomit-covered clothes in a freezer bag
missing the poetry reading because I'd lost my voice
attending the poetry reading the day my boyfriend broke up with me
Mary Gaitskill said she liked my glasses in 2007
Home Alone VHS tape Xmas present
my aunt wanted to take me to Kokomo, Ind.
I thought she meant from the Beach Boys song
being the flower girl at my parents' wedding
eating Swedish meatballs from Gordon Food Service
staying with my grandma while my parents honeymooned in Vegas
writing 250 words on why spitting is bad
looking at the ducklings in the courtyard through the classroom window
ten years later my 1st grade teacher's hair gone from gray to brown
my 6th grade social studies teacher dead of cancer
she taught the girls' sex ed curriculum and defined the term "bowel movement"
being a Barbie for Halloween in kindergarten
nearly meeting Michael Martone so many times it's like we're friends
the school counselor who took me to see my mom in the hospital
his teenage daughter dead from leukemia a few years later

watching the OJ verdict in school
disallowed from the field trip bus with movies for well-behaved children
disallowed from watching *Fern Gully: The Last Rainforest*
smashed in the face with a plastic lunchbox
said he thought I was a boy but the lunchbox swung on his wrist
kayaking on the East Race with my grandpa once
dumping a lunch tray over onto my feet
chicken and noodles on my new curly laces
tripping on my way to receive an award at a gymnasium ceremony
the Burger King coupon or Pizza Hut Book-It program hologram stickers
burying the for-sale sign in my friend's front yard with snow
burning board game pieces in the bathroom sink
someone's older sister putting makeup on me at a sleepover
my mother burning my forehead with the curling iron before photos at Olan Mills
ducking down in the backseat not to be seen in the Kmart parking lot
walking the last block to my friend's house so she wouldn't see the ugly van my mom drov
conjuring Bloody Mary in the elementary school girls' room
my 5th grade teacher saying "electronic mail"
being too young for softball
playing tee ball with the little girls while my classmates learned to pitch
forced to wear adult size large t-shirts through adolescence
told I asked great-grandma "Why do you have so many wrinkles?"
told I opened all the Xmas presents and said "Where are the rest?"
collecting the pouches of spare buttons off the ladies' blouses in the department store
driving a scooter straight into a fence while my mom videotaped
allegedly shoplifting a baby monkey stuffed animal from the drugstore
accused of cheating in a reading speed contest
accused of tracing in a drawing contest
boy on the playground ripping off my necklace
smashing my glasses into my face on the parallel bars
shutting my thumb in the bathroom stall door
when we had to hold them closed for each other
shutting my thumb in the car door
skinning my knees in my 20s

getting lost in the woods in Virginia while I could hear the highway
losing my boyfriend's debit card
an old man doctor telling me he can remove my acne scars
making friends to play with their toys or be close to their mothers
the gym teacher tracking our periods with a clipboard
to force us to take our panties off in the shower
anonymously reported to the guidance counselor for suspected anorexia twice
bit in the face by a dog while playing Mike Tyson's Punch-Out
asking my mom to sell my New Kids on the Block tickets
because I couldn't handle how excited I was
asked in the carpool if mine was a 'university family'

Cruel Simulations

my wrong argument, a diagonal
a little depressed, my syntax
the apologia of my revolution

my not-knowing, an island not to scale
a little grammatical, my machismo
the futility of my antibiotics

my discomfort, a Leo-Virgo cusp baby
a little status quo, my violence
the anxiety of my talk

my caution, a nauseous maw
a little problematic, my allergens
the depth of my pelvic floor

my force, a financier in seersucker
a little crowdsourced, my oaths
the adequacy of my occupation

my idea, a boom generator
a little pointed, my design
the externality of my solitude

my gentrification, a curb appeal
a little nostalgic, my irony
the path of my underemployment

my status, a part-time appointment
a little chez moi, my cuisine
the layover of my dirtwind

my best me, an enthusiasm
a little automatic, my disability
the white glove of my heart

my freshest article, a new yes
a little tolerant, my pedagogy
the academics of my mobility

my white-tailed doe, a natural loss
a little real-life, my reservations
the androgyny of my crankshaft

my autoerotic subjectivity, unmediated
a little economic, my aboutness
the girth of my decency

my abject sensitivity, legitimate
a little arch, my femininity
the flexibility of my access

Field Notes, Oaxaca

*

Beauty is a ploy.
Beauty is added at the marketing stage.
Beauty is proof she is fit to consume.

The body must come from certain areas.
The body must come from in-demand elsewhere.
The body must truly be called.

A village of small-scale producers.
A village boasts dozens of houses.
A village imparts a particular character.

She is highly varied.
She is certified for use.
She competes in international markets.

*

Beauty is a nautral misconception.
Beauty began as a gimmick.
Beauty produces for the party market.

Rituals of scorpion: do not recommend.
Rituals of salt or orange slices.
Rituals of before breakfast in the north.

The producers represent her as a premium.
The producers view her in relation to brandy.
The producers offer a selection but don't mix.

The misconception continues.
The misconception can control diseases.
The misconception is an aphrodisiac.

*

The state sponsors the annual festival.
The state sponsors a number of entrepreneurs.
The state sponsors a variety of export products.

Sold in 27 countries on 3 continents.
Sold every year in the capital city.
Sold by promoting handcrafted quality.

Agencies obtain the equipment needed.
Agencies promote the culture associated.
Agencies can sample and buy a large variety.

Locals and tourists can strongly participate.
Locals and tourists help small producers.
Locals and tourists in the last decade or so obtain.

*

Can be used as antiseptic, dilute eyewash.
Can be used in combination with salt.
Can be used to reduce oxidation.

Protect the precious surface.
Protect fire jugglers and spinners.
Protect furnace linings and ceramics.

Considered safe for household kitchens.
Considered in a gel form and injectable paste.
Considered especially toxic to infants.

Beauty has a slow elimination rate.
Beauty dissolves to make fire green.
Beauty can lead to an arrest of previous power.

A Certain Profit Situation

Now the gold supply at Fort Knox has reached a critical level, and something must be done.

American citizens cannot own gold.

This in itself tends to aggravate the dollar drain and bring the moment of reckoning closer.

How can the individual protect himself against an improvident government which has become caught in such a financial tangle?

The ideal speculation is one in which the risk is small and the possible profit large, and so no better speculation can ever be found.

The simplest way to own gold is by buying stock in a producing gold mine.

With that kind of potential profit, it is almost mandatory to own at least a little gold, even if the change should be delayed for some years.

This is a certain profit situation, and it will repeat itself annually until the price of gold is finally raised.

Dear, Dear, Dear

What I dread // a locked door // Complex I am meant to decode
when my default is refusal // Manichean, my conditional love
wants transparent blankness // A privacy workaround // I lose it

Favor disobedience if authority is the State only // I move across
the street bound for home and hope you are there with a new word
to dissolve // Eartha Kitt says *compromise* like a joke // Bring your bags

Take your things in and unpack // can we be good // can I pull
threads with my hands while you talk // if I retrace my steps more
problems emerge that had been well buried // You don't agree

I put my suit on and go to work // The opposition to our opposition
says we are impure // That is our point // All the dead children
Anonymous posts photos of // A promise to work together next time

We set a goal // but I hemmorhage money privately // American adults
typing *I feel homeless* with impunity // While the office is recarpeted
My love is still a big map // A legend // I keep a little secret

An American Poem

I dreamed Eileen Myles told me I was dressing too sexy. She said all my tops were transparent and I was distracting the men from their work.

Then a hurricane came and we were in the greenhouse area of a Walmart, waiting for my mother to choose a planter of purple flowers. The storm was coming and we (me, the cashier, my mother, Eileen Myles, and two ladies in line behind us) were all going to drown in a tidal surge.

My mother wouldn't choose. No one was impatient. We all behaved like what we were: tiny little workers without power.

From a Wedding

In it we are between acts
Waiting for an arrival
A perfectly-timed entrance
by a perfect coif, dye job

It is all fine
Together among performers
A woman says "I am a professional"
though everyone could tell

We stand in a big circle
the decision long-since made

If you can forget the government
The idea is starting over by choice

In this scene our job is to wait

Field Notes, Brooklyn

That girl and I will always be cool with each other   Wrong again

            Rugburn from climbing around on the roof

                no, not historical Williamsburg

Disqualified   Bar guy let me read his divorce papers   Sighing along

           Ruin it   watch me   Alone and I don't

She calls right when I'm roasting an eggplant   Spotted

in the bike lane smoking a cigarette   I forgot

      It's all demand   normal guy looking for an amazing girl

I'm moaning at the new colors of Le Creuset cookware   Now that I've gotten

          everyone to leave me alone   trying to organize

Fashion Blast Quarter

Young film comes again

      Color the image away

It mutes love   Color gets thought

      It mentions hours

Absent the sapphire   All the wet birds and webs

      Blackout anomaly

         Away tundra, away marble

Her private conversation foregrounded

              She found your drawing

Next spring the supplicants will

         learn to tell time

Practice on her

Clothes communicate

the gum of a shell   What is that

Get selection

Get lungs

A small example   Returns are growing

You mentioned *aspire*

Bring me   sparkling wishes

the Playboy jet

a whole universal and hovering body

Or just please hurt me

Overlapping and mean at the palace where

Ideal metals make a hostile sound

In reference to the wrong part of music

Material fills the interstices

A string tied around your finger to remember

The swizzle stick is blue glass

If you are alone   just keep swizzling

Take thoughts to the lake   and dump them in

Noise at the end of a record

When the tone arm hiccups

Rescue it

A string tied around your finger to remember

Punk rock's selection criteria   Keep showing up

      Run in the gutter   Your dirtiest self

You can't leave it   Curb alert

      Fight against a blessing   Past surface

                I wanna be around

Friday night   I wanna be   Hammer and saw make

      Maybe a background accident   The tape said

Just keep swizzling   It is all *accident*

      Bear with me now   Put it on ice

A string tied around your finger to remember

Some bird on a branch is losing its mind

        Your golden hoop earrings   Tight around your skin

          Ligaments have memory

    and want to shake

In distress   Often out of rhythm   No sequence

        The dragonfly will sew up your lips

Your eyes   Your thirst for muddy fields

Touch the hoop

      Flick it

Like a ladybug   A firefly

       Go to nature then

Into someone else's struggle

No one's a suffragette   It's an obsolete technology

Intent on tape delay   If you don't have a hard drive

That's okay

Pass around source notes like a joint

Beautiful and fulfilled

Obviously high

Courtship traces vectors in bloodstains

An adult doesn't facefuck on an empty stomach

What do you call that game

You flinched   It's a stopgap sex act

Snow bank

Delivery room

A place the mind can go alone

Cover up gaps in memory with a joke

Adults have relationships

Nice work   Blank or just muted

Down with the contemporary dimension

My name   I don't entertain

If you came here for a story   Put this in your mouth

Count backward from a hundred

Mathematical skin, bloom view

       Allegiant body transcribes sentiments

          Development through chatter

      Plastic market   Take sunset, antiquity leaves

         Escape speech falters

Despite dimness of philosophical sense in the interval

      Door glances   subvert polite comportment

        Person with two passports

     Return to the intrigue in scene

Lyric series describes a false sky

        No thought when the world lightens

          Drive the surface empire forward

Society paces within stalls   Normalizes the hollow

        Choir of resigned women in concert matinee

Accurate construction arose   A communistic design

            Geraniums in bloom

                    Graph of tweed paradise

Emblematic manifesto of inchoate bitterness

                A poor imitation of humanism

       Her sense   curious about multivalence

            Should warn

Feminine dialect a known function   for sentimental recovery

Treasures dumped out on porches

Abandoned strip mine of yard sale referents

        The gray market riot over toys or something

Therefore   the lava and tide games

Thought we invented playing at avoidance

        Establishing a context for the problem

Holes are

        abstract pleasures   if you didn't know

They give direction   to feeling

        The Cadillac of fake pee kits

Water-drunk at the drug test facility

Eclipsed   trailheads

I still worry my body is too childish

    for the lightning fields   to sleep near another

      I don't get invited to weddings

Breath   once spoken

Overflows   Manages to tease

This conversation is over

      Your hand sanitizer is in the backpack

    You don't want to get involved

    With arm's-length negotiation

      a lot of shit will never happen

Gin Jury

I get away with my abuse, and
the bad leaves. Beg an invitation,
a monster. Spray orange scent
as if to trick this gloom. Instead,
burn to heat. The clean house
is regrettable. Chicago, where you
ask for help. A vacuum dissolves
candy. I eat the boundaries
because I know the innocent
want my throat. I wish you'd say
I can't see. You give and mirror.

Pronoun Kettling

Image of a rose-lighted flank is revealed, woman in the shape
of a girl becomes space and a doll consists of a line between
things. The line moves from a lighted boundary at which misty
light calls. Ghost limb determines that (existing in air) the witch
relates to I pronoun, whiteness moved downward. Her selvage
is slow, bleeds. Her control like boy-pulls-an-animal or
boy-watches-a-mouse. A water tank sits, a truly panoramic material.
The sun distributes its surface of visibility onto desert audience.
A real man substitutes for beauty of trill note. Danger is: you'll be
dream's intermediary. Unraveling event of friendship opens and
foreign woman radiates in a loved one's face. A plane tips up.
Light is not real. *Film image is so cerebral*, he thinks directional.
Linking is flow among screens, which are windows, the photograph
so handsome with instinct for self-preservation. One thing more
disconnected: your monologue stripped down.

Nothing A Magnetic Black

Everything gets killed.

Get me to the church on time.

Joyride to your grave.   Wait.

Commute to your wedding.   Stop.   End it there.

Go ahead, be a dead girl. C'est normal.

Relax.

Purring your way in.   Domesticity kills.

Zero gravity saves in a secular zone.

Your success is viable.   It's got legs.

Getting past your failure by getting on the horn.

What the noun is is a very early educated guess,

but it's not the man I voted for.   You made a noun with free will.

We don't have that kind of time.

Gray market in the shadow state.

Black the black that expands.

White a white which shrinks.

Black is a color, an organizing principle flagged for investigation.

Your tabula rasa my panacea.   Get down on it.

Everything a dead girl participates in.

Not recognizable what I live through.

All the parts a partner would touch.

Nothing your maleness can't expand.

The lukewarm bath was supposed to help me.

What's the message?   We sold it.

What's the message?

It was for sale.

A compliment.   An insult.

Your happy feelings.

We all hope you never find out

what collaboration happens in the astral plane.

Your decision is a judgment like finally.

But a decision is a loss.   Unresolved.

They really think we've got the world under control.

They trust us with their loot.

                         Get me to the lazy river on time.

          The only bathtub big enough to be satisfying.

                              I look down at my legs,

           how foreign they seem.

                     Mary Ruefle warned me success would ultimately be
                                        unsatisfying.

              Dead spider on my bar of soap so

don't touch me after all.   Hand me a plane ticket, a t-shirt, nothing please

          with sexy lace trim.   Into the vague.

Space expands whether they are scars or wrinkles, big or small.

          Into the black, and it isn't about color.

          Into the dark and it is.

Mary said

I'll be the one who looks very sad.

At the airport.

Time resolves unless you're the dead girl.

And what a problem.

None of My Business

Listen at the walls to learn neighbor's habits because there is a great deal to observe.
No such thing as a secret. I go to sleep and wake up and still my partner is not home,
so I lose sleep over what a good listener I can't help but be.

I am sick in the night stumbling into the bathroom and no one wakes to my sound.
If I weren't alone with the idea of separate lives.
If I felt safe enough in sleep to lie down once until the next day.

In the kitchen with a praying mantis I panicked and crushed it. With the water shut off,
he made pancakes with a gallon jug of water while I cried with the neighbor's girlfriend.
It's a pattern of behavior: I annex satisfaction.

Heels click outside the window. Sighs slip through the wall that used to be a doorway,
and I start napping in my office on campus. You drink too much, you stay too long.
That's why they call it a party. Not enough night for me.

Pole Position

Repeating ad infinitim the same message about success

Palmed off congratulation on the immigrant mouth

A turn-on

True worry into a nook

Becomes forgery

Becomes a triple negative

He doesn't know his own value

Smooth vague weeknights with seamstress and martyr

Listen

Redundancy built in

Glissando, basic plagiarism

For demonstration's sake

Shiny penny, no one cares

Negative net worth garners faith

Top-ranking rat bastard goes to the greenest thumb

A shift in position is worse than random

An idea that makes a joke of itself

The law says not to get caught

Lest you get your babyfat pinched

Home Economics

Into evening I crept, I crept, I
discovered I was afraid.

I watch a woman wave to a ferry boat on the Hudson River. I watch a little
girl wave to a dog. Keep your hard-luck story to yourself. Hoboken flips
me the bird all summer.

Material conditions include: time into money, money into a meal.
Measuring feed as for any animal on a diet and a budget.

Into evening I crept, I crept, I
entered a place like having a lawn,
not a place like think of your goal.
House with cars in the drive,
place like a yank to force it right.

The home economy keeps humming. I must thank illegal immigration
and white flight. Manual transmission a matter of freedom in blizzard,
a sick mother requires extra care.

They want me to come back and fix it. Leaves burn in small fires
up and down the road. The road bends away.
The road feels like another.

Into evening I crept, I crept, I
wrote leaving in the past tense.
Into space like save a life, it may be your own.
No cash. No trust. Like work, a deli,
a polo. *Get them dogs running*—blood does
not run as fast as I did.

Into evening I crept, I crept, I
forced into the agora, out of structure for labor.
That will always have been. After burden
broaches cusp of harmful, I force again.
This time must get well. Force get well soon.

A brother-in-law garners all the new leaf funding. Call it a loan and
laugh. The little old ladies who outlive their friends survive on
having also outlived a need for caution.

Who is left after a century of emergencies and traffic? Together,
they take an exercise walk down the cul-de-sac and, obviously, back.

Field Notes, Liverpool

Female bodies are typically designed at human scale
Female bodies are established on a roof or in an atrium
Female bodies are subject to the constraints of convention

The front may be a formal and semi-public body
The front may also be on a balcony or in windowboxes
The front is the most common form

She is in proximity to a residence
She is typically found in community
She is most often intended for pleasure

May feature structures, such as those for exhibiting
May feature growing herbs and vegetables
May feature special features, such as rockery or water

*

Surface is often the site of romantic interest
Surface is public bodies associated with parks
Surface accompanies reproductions of lyrical architecture

These usually include several dozen talents
These cultivate styles mentioned in literary works
These are walkways and benches and a weather-resistant bust

Signs can mark locations for outdoor weddings
Signs near her usually provide relevant quotations
Signs are an important element of sustainability

Typical amenities are herbaceous profusion or
Typical geometric layout, one of either or
Typical signs with charming dividers

*

Mothering used restrained designs
Mothering goes back many centuries, but
Mothering uses more structured Victorian materials

She uses a mixture of ornamental and edible features
She, with massed beds of brilliant color,
She selects an informal dense arrangement

Rather than grandeur and formal structure
Rather than 1870s England in response
Rather than depending on grace and charm

The bodies were more select
The bodies' popularity grew
The bodies more casual by design

*

Modern books emphasized the importance and value of
Modern ones include countless regional and personal variations
Modern shes of the more traditional motherly body

Influenced by the series of thematic books,
influenced by the importance and value of natural birth,
influenced those in Europe and the United States

The earliest were far more practical than the modern
The earliest with an emphasis on vegetables and herbs
The earliest with even livestock if time allowed

Theory became more dominant, with fruit trees
Theory was beehives, and
Theory came along over time

The Courage of Excess

Draping the body
with a garland
of banners
cobwebs
flowers
ivy
ribbons
vines.

Decoration like
tattoos: permanent
makeup. Building
a personal brand
based on having
the most
flavor crystals.
The courage
to sport bling but
love swagger.

Encouraging
obsession
is solving a problem
by holding a laptop
up over your head.
Over your head
is a dangerous place
to put your body.

Encouraging obsession
is a blunt force trauma.
A *Law & Order* type mentality.
Street justice, country grammar.
What's brave about that:
no one paid for it.

Several Advantages As Areas For Policy Analysis / Social Action, As Regards Living In A Corporate Bank

*

Corporate banks are common,
and perhaps close to universal,
since most people
in urbanized areas
would probably consider themselves
to be living in one.

*

Successful corporate bank investment
frequently requires
little specialized technical skill,
and often little or no money.
Investment may call
for an investment of time,
but material costs are often low.

*

With corporate bank investment,
compared to activity on larger scales,
results are more likely to be visible
and quickly forthcoming. The streets
are cleaner; the crosswalk is painted;
the trees are planted; the festival
draws a crowd.

*

Visible and swift results
are indicators of success;
and since success is reinforcing,
the probability of subsequent
corporate bank investment
is increased.

*

Because corporate bank investment
usually involves others, such investments
create or strengthen connections and relationships
with other banks, leading in turn to a variety
of potentially positive effects,
often hard to predict.

Software Kill Switch

In high school I read a recommendation letter written for me and it said I didn't have talent, but I was very committed.

I worked for a small company and because I answered the phone the other employees thought I wasn't as smart as them.

I am telling you I figured out how to survive by treading water until the next thing came up.

My manager ripped my shirt open at the party and then walked away. I had my first shot of bourbon in a souffle cup // a plastic cuplette for a side of ranch dressing // he wore a hat that said SERIAL KILLER and I wanted to fuck him but I didn't.

Someone was trying to make me feel guilty, lying to catch me lying, and I wasn't going to let that work.

I got a urinary tract infection just from being too busy waiting tables to pee.

Pace is a drive by force I can muster, the real work started when I'd get home. When I was working 60 hours a week, my dad seemed to like hearing about it. He saw my first apartment and was sad for me.

I had a good boss and a bad boss
and I promised not to write about the work
even after my non-compete clause
expired. I still haven't: I try to confirm
the deep state in casual conversation
but no one takes it seriously—
a conspiracy theory I could prove.

Five years earlier, another boss said my
reign of terror
was coming to an end. Rock steady.
We began to rock. Movement under
a radar, any radar, any year, and
a pivot that terminates the era.

Scarcity Creates Fetishes

No need to perform a language stunt.
Fear of peak oil your check engine light freakout.
Smearing the bike chain across leather interior.
Tired of being the wrong thing at the wrong place.

Sometimes I go all day without putting my thinking cap on.
I am a very careful blank target in a shitty emergency.
I don't know how to reset the terms since I
think everyone who has sex with me likes me.

If I want to talk about materialism, I'll say the word.
Wait, the need to safeguard against trends is here.
"Your thinking cap!" Mother said, "That's so old-fashioned!"
If behavior modification is too hard, try not being the slayer.

The New Look

It's vintage journalist.
Porkpie hat. Stylized, but
nothing you see in the
magazines anymore. The look
is skinny and busy.

Dress so
revolutionary when not
leaning for help. The down-
and-out take note, imagine
kinship with your basic
plainness.

People look at your clothes in the city.

Youth excuses some behaviors,
but the hot heat aggression
doesn't relent. The look
draws negative attention.

Deadeye stare, or blank ahead
when catcaller says. When to push it.

There is what you wear
and then there is your body,
which you are also held
accountable for.

A man in a hat must be considered
on a case-by-case basis.

I think I can't scream,
then something scary
happens and a scream
comes out. I surprise
myself and the rat
on the sidewalk.

My roommate
borrows my sandals and
says "I feel like a lesbian!"
Your look gets digested
by the audience.

No One Goes Fading That Fast

House and factory sanitized to provide
avoidance zone. The known spaces

that however fucked are familiar.
When you decide, I hope you find the negation

leaving feels like. Surviving
looks like bailing. Here all busy

with the looking, bumming around.
Around what? An opening. I'm attempting

to model function, so threats loom
near. Venue has value too, but does not

count on absence. See what age looks like
on a face regionally. We don't argue

about family anymore. Nice how home remains
useful for healing wounds. Take the busy

schedule to the clinic with the other
symptoms. Reminded not to waste. No—

warned against it though my expenses
are no longer on their worry radar.

The fade of deprivation. When I've
accepted as much as I can, I cross over

to a movement called Occupy Time.
A girly girl misunderstood, thought it was

idleness. The structure will have
to return and return and continue.

It will have to pierce as it loops,
make an alloy. I have a new weapon

called a cracked mirror, or I forget
what. A list of demands, a prior

engagement. Rings on a tree stump.
A pocketful of beautiful vitamins.

Romeo + Juliet Poem

Let's watch each other die. Repeat. Let's watch
each other die and repeat it in a loop.
I am having what you might call a hard time
with what's happened. The light turns
to bubbles turns to pool water turns to
champagne and we are in swimsuits splashing.

Let's lose a lot of blood in the rain during
a misunderstanding. I am wearing a tasteful
glitter bra I made myself, and have to use both
hands to pull up the car window glass.
This is as soft core as it gets. So star-crossed
I can't take credit, the same song over.

A cloud of silver confetti marks the night
as significant in case anyone missed the cues.
If my coping mechanism doesn't work for you,
give it up. You do shots of bourbon, I'll pretend
I'm Nick Cave. Let's shut up and dance.
Let's down tune and get grindcore.

People will talk, but it's not overwrought
if I actually melt. Because all the girls
in flipflops watch how you move, it was about
you from the start. Today is a lost one
and we will only catnap in adjacent rooms.
What happened was you knew you'd ask

what happened and that didn't stop you.
Let's touch despite the new rule you made up.
Let's burp in each other's faces since we had

the same thing for dinner. Instead of finding
words for it, we hardly. Don't even. We pass out
without filling up the hot tub. Blue light.

I want to say *you always look so cool* but I keep
my mouth shut. My only love: whatever
is set before me. And everyone knows.
Dramatic irony remix in which you don't know I
know you know—well, let's turn the subwoofer
all the way up and sleep in bodysound.

Desire seeks an object and reason is not
a consideration. Come at me, sweet pea.
Come at me, sweat stain. The end is far off still,
but I'm sure you're not the Christ figure.
I get the tab because I live in a city. A jar gets
loosened, tightened, loosened again.

Conceptualism is Dead

Charlie Day, little bear cub, come bite my lip.
I love every thing I've never touched.

When the child was a child, he put
everything to his lips. A cause célèbre.

My diet of labor-intensive collage is
the art installation child of my heart.

I am basically begging for it, but it is
the revolution not what you imagine I need.

I've a curatorial vision for my favorite flavor.
Colleagues are policing with compassion.

Hell is around the corner—temper, temper.
Your big bad superlatives meet my best twist.

Frenemy

Social means celebration means looking happy. Great but not special. I'd say the
same thing about anyone who wasn't myself.

Your tragicomic gluten sensitivity is what graduate school was good for.

I grind my teeth so hard they're getting shorter. Singsong litany of friction
malfunctions: teeth to jaw to neck & shoulders.

The embarrassment of riches is leverage, counterweight to upper-upper body.

You can bite through your pinky finger as easily as a baby carrot. Women-
workers are making do without an ergonomic chair to squat in.

Lockjaw as adjective, as in your lockjaw pedagogy or lockjaw stag trippant.

It's constructive criticism to point out that probiotics and antibiotics should
cancel out. Let's see your announcement.

Rescue Narrative

One home rescued, one home thrown away
One town jubilant, one erased and plowed

Flag-waving never goes out of fashion
The news has a story about a cargo ship

Three women, all of whom ran blue for hours
The crowd held tightly father's waist

One sundae, two spoons. High humor, family
vacation dynamic—I'm the dull sister

Disagree with my heroic interpretation of time
Get back home, your fence adorned with prayers

Favorite meal, favorite undisclosed town for sale
Not for long—One place saved, the rest so small

Wife Fight

Adult acne in all four seasons
I should've maybe only said about 10% of that

Using a wife's face cream, I get caught
It is shared privately but I can see it

He does a silly voice sometimes
The smell of my old room

On a generative meetup
For little bitty pip culture

You will need a helper
Not to say money is a defect

Academic conference on kink
Like a spanking panel—okay

Shit like that kept bumming me out
Rapidly approaching excellence

An embarrassment of Tuesday chances
Dead today—a wife on an April breeze

We get on the airplane
No room for me and I just take it

Facility pen pal feels ashamed
Xed out and taking it in repose

So looking in horror is mode
A la mode de la crème hear me

Pennies on the Dollar

If a person cannot admit making a mistake, he should not buy in to currency trading.

There is always someone willing to take on currency trading, but the price may be disappointing.

Many investors are seeking the illusion of security through their profits.

Only monies which can afford to be lost should be used in such ventures for the entire capital can disappear with disquieting rapidity.

Two such opportunities:
1. New machines were described that could recognize and give change for paper money.
2. An invention that, if it worked, would certainly require a long educational campaign to persuade women to use it, and there might very well be dangerous side effects which would prevent it from ever going into practical use.

Speculation, therefore, cannot be successfully carried on by the dabbler.

A glamorous new invention or process associated with currency trading will move up many multiples in price as a result.

The coin represented utility and security.

The bogie of financial emergencies has been greatly overdone. Cash can be removed in a matter of three days.

I Don't Want to Talk About My Problems

I get so emotional baby when I set my iTunes to shuffle
I walk down your street but not on purpose, let you know
in case you want to hang with me
I'm at a birthday party
I just peed with my backpack on and felt like an animal
There's a cute bartender here too bad you're not here

My heart pumps out real objects
I have to show you because sensations are parasitic
My love will destroy me if I don't let it out
A humiliation like any old public disease
Here it is, just exactly like I knew it would look
My love repeats *It's never too late* and I can't quiet it

Disregard the pleading, it was part of my process
In the back of the theater for the spaghetti western
I want to know when you think about me
Found a phone charger at the bar and just took it
It's the anniversary of something in my life tonight
I could be talked into moving almost anywhere

I'm eating sopressata and watching softball
This is not for my benefit
Low-grade kindness is white noise to a socialite
I could learn the habit of not acknowledging
Anyway it's been really fun getting to know you
Déjà vu is possibly narcissism, which is garbage

Love is the Plan

I give a little help for you plus something new
And a little more until my now is cracked

Look at what mess I made of it trying to be good
The game limits how often you renew

When victory was in me, you would think of him
Once you question what replacement will

What departures our dialogue will open, my dear
We are sad in a post office kissing in front of strangers

We are hiding from the soldiers—why always
No one will take the world away from you

I only want to not feel ugly in it taking firm steps
I don't mind your debt—the plan is death

Giant Octopus

If it were my poem, I'd start with the death of the mother.
She unblocks the cave and collapses dead in the opening.

Then working backward, her labor in arranging the eggs alone in the cave underwater.
After receiving the sperm in neatly delivered packets, she stores it in her undercarriage.

But both lovers die, separated by labor.
The beginning and the end.
My bones pop.

I said I don't want to be the educator and she said but you are.

I Got Among Them

// Politer, I honor

Among counterfeit //

I told him

I've been told

Of graciously begged

Of stray appetites

I've been told I cure and hide

and show a little stark fancy

To this I was silent //

That unteachable wild rat

Pleasures his naked propensity

To appear, and his reader consented

// All manner of unnatural howl

To spurn was to master

A show

I told them all   I came near

And I told and I told

NOTES

"Pain Theory" reworks a line Maggie Nelson cites in her essay "Great to Watch," which appears in *The Art of Cruelty* (Norton, 2011). She records a sentence in her notebook from Ryan Trecartin's 2007 video *I-Be Area*: "My personal really concise pussy is developing a very inner monologue which I will not reveal to you as I become dynamic."

"Field Notes, Brooklyn" owes itself to Soda Bar in Brooklyn.

"Fashion Blast Quarter" owes itself to Mei-Mei Berssenbrugge's *I Love Artists*.

"Several Advantages" owes itself to the Wikipedia page for neighborhood.

"Field Notes, Oaxaca" owes itself to the Wikipedia page for mezcal.

"Field Notes, Liverpool" owes itself to the Wikipedia page for garden.

"Wife Fight" includes statements uttered by Anselm Berrigan.

"A Certain Profit Situation" and "Pennies on the Dollar" borrow text from *Anyone Can Make a Million* by Morton Schulman (Bantam Books, 1968), which I found in my room at VCCA in January 2013.

Krystal Languell was born in South Bend, Indiana. She is the author of the book *Call the Catastrophists* (BlazeVox, 2011) and four chapbooks: *Last Song* (dancing girl press, 2014), *Be a Dead Girl* (Argos Books, 2014), *Fashion Blast Quarter* (Flying Object, 2014), and *Diamonds in the Flesh* (Double Cross Press, 2015). From 2011-2015, she conducted interviews with women poets, culminating in the publication of *Archive Theft* (Essay Press, 2015). Her poetry has been anthologized in *Read Women* (Locked Horn Press, 2015) and *Best of the Web* (Dzanc Books, 2010), and she has received a Poetry Project Emerge-Surface-Be fellowship (2013-2014) and a Lower Manhattan Cultural Council workspace residency (2014-2015). Development Director for Belladonna* Collaborative and publisher of the feminist poetry journal *Bone Bouquet*, Languell also works as a freelance bookkeeper for small presses and teaches at Pratt Institute in Brooklyn, New York.

Titles from 1913 Press:

Arcane Rituals from the Future by Leif Haven (2016, selected by Claudia Rankine)
I, Too, Dislike It by Mia You (2016, Editrice's Pick)
Unlikely Conditions by Cynthia Arrieu-King & Hillary Gravendyk (2016)
Abra by Amaranth Borsuk & Kate Durbin (2016)
Pomme & Granite by Sarah Riggs (2015)
Untimely Death is Driven Out Beyond the Horizon by Brenda Iijima (2015)
Full Moon Hawk Application by CA Conrad (Assless Chaps, 2014)
Big House/Disclosure by Mendi & Keith Obadike (2014)
Four Electric Ghosts by Mendi & Keith Obadike (2014)
O Human Microphone by Scott McFarland (2014, selected by Rae Armantrout)
Kala Pani by Monica Mody (2013)
Bravura Cool by Jane Lewty (2012, selected by Fanny Howe)
The Transfer Tree by Karena Youtz (2012)
Conversities by Dan Beachy-Quick & Srikanth Reddy (2012)
Home/Birth: A Poemic by Arielle Greenberg & Rachel Zucker (2011)
Wonderbender by Diane Wald (2011)
Ozalid by Biswamit Dwibedy (2010)
Sightings by Shin Yu Pai (2007)
Seismosis by John Keene & Christopher Stackhouse (2006)

Read 1-6, an annual anthology of inter-translation, Sarah Riggs & Cole Swensen, eds.
1913 a journal of forms, Issues 1-6, Sandra Doller, ed.

Forthcoming:

Conversations Over Stolen Food by Jon Cotner & Andy Fitch
Strong Suits, Brad Flis
Old Cat Lady: A Love Story in Possibilities by Lily Hoang
Hg, the liquid by Ward Tietz
x/she: stardraped by Laura Vena (selected by John Keene)
A Turkish Dictionary by Andrew Wessels (Editrixes' Pick)
Lucy 72 by Ronaldo V. Wilson

1913 titles are distributed by Small Press Distribution: www.spdbooks.org

"The critics who usually are willing enough to play the part of beacon light, were singularly unilluminating."

-*The New York Times,* 1913